A Time to
PRAY

A Time to
PRAY

ELAINE BOND

CREATION
HOUSE
A STRANG COMPANY

A Time to Pray by Elaine Bond
Published by Creation House
A Strang Company
600 Rinehart Road
Lake Mary, Florida 32746
www.creationhouse.com

Cover design by Terry Clifton

Library of Congress Control Number: 2007924903
International Standard Book Number: 978-1-59979-202-6

First Edition

07 08 09 10 11 — 9 8 7 6 5 4 3 2 1
Printed in the United States of America

Contents

Why I Love to Pray

"ELAINE, THANK YOU FOR teaching me how to pray," was the parting comment from each of three dear friends as we hugged farewell. I was returning to my home province of Ontario, Canada, after living for fifteen years in beautiful British Columbia. This was the first time they had ever said this. "How have I taught anyone to pray?" I wondered.

Now, ten years later, God has put it on my heart to write this little book. At first I felt the same way—puzzled. *What can I possibly say about prayer*?

My idea of a person who should write a book on prayer would be Rees Howells, who changed the events of the Second World War through his prayers. George Mueller, who saw to the daily provisions for hundreds of orphans through prayer, would be another logical choice.

As I reflected on my friends' comments, I realized that

I had not taught them how to pray, but I had imparted to them my deep love for prayer. This is much like what I do when helping single moms in the area of homemaking. I impart to women a love for their children and home.

I know why I love parenting and homemaking: it is focusing my efforts into something that brings life-long rewards. You may laugh and think, "Now, how does doing our laundry bring a lifelong reward?" Maybe clean clothes don't bring the reward, but serving someone you love can, especially if you serve them long enough to make a difference.

You may not see the fruit of your labor when your inquisitive toddler is yanking the laundry out of the basket faster than you can put it into the drawers. It may not be when the middle of the bedroom floor is the closest the dirty clothes gets to the laundry basket for a fast-paced teen.

But as you teach them by example, you will eventually see your children grow up and begin to serve others—a reflection of your attitude in the home. The little things you do in life have a lasting effect. I always remember what my high school Latin teacher said before exams, "It is the little words that will fail you."

It isn't the laundry that brings the reward; it is your willingness to do the mundane to *benefit* someone you love. Delegating the tasks as children get older is also showing your love!

But this is a book about prayer, not homemaking. So why do I love to pray so much? I love to pray for the same reason

I love homemaking. I know that my praying will bring life-long rewards. Lives are changed through my willingness to spend time doing something that I enjoy.

Some may view prayer as a task as boring as doing the laundry. But for me it is not my laundry that I love, but my children. It is not prayer that I love, but the lives touched.

Moms, if I can impart to you the love of prayer or somehow deepen your experience in prayer, it will help you more than anything. And you can even be an instrument of change in the world outside of your own four walls.

There was a moment one day when it all began—that is, my longing to spend time in prayer. It amazes me every time I think of it.

Chapter 2

Happy Birthday!

THERE ARE TIMES IN our lives when we become reflective. My thirty-second birthday, a long time ago, was one of those times for me.

By then I had been a single parent for four years. Amy, my eldest, was seven years old, and Natalie was five. We lived in a tiny home in a beautiful location overlooking the ocean. There were lush gardens and fruit trees in the yard. Even on a gray November day, the scenery was lovely. This home was truly a little gem and one I hoped to keep, so I had made the owners a rent-to-purchase offer. I also owned and operated a ladies' consignment shop in town. I was happy in my new surroundings, starting life over far away from all that was familiar.

It was the evening of my birthday and all was quiet. My little girls were tucked in their beds and sleeping soundly. I put another log in the fireplace and curled up on the big overstuffed couch—far too large for my small living room, but way too comfy to depart with for appearance.

Snuggled in with just my thoughts to keep me company, I started to reflect about my life. After all, I was thirty-two today! As I pondered, I sensed an unexplainable yearning inside of me. I couldn't quite identify it as anything more than possible dissatisfaction with something in my life.

After high school, I went to teachers' college, yet here I was operating a clothing store for employment. When I first became a single parent, I ran a day care. In the evenings I took a real estate course, hoping to improve income through a new home business. I graduated from the program with very good marks—the highest in my class. I attribute that not to my great intelligence, but to the incredible amount of concentration it took to study with children always under-foot. However, after only four months I realized that real estate as a career creates a huge time demand, rather than the flexibility I was seeking. For the sake of my children, I quit.

Now, on my birthday, I was looking at my career history. I had my teaching certificate, a real estate license, and now my business as a proprietress.

Next I thought about my hobbies. I had several over the years but was not really good at any of them. The hobby of one year gave way to a new one the following year. They were a source of relaxation, but could not hold my interest long enough for me to truly master them.

Music? Just ask my girls, who painfully endured my desire

to play a guitar. I could not even master tuning the instrument. My guitar was collecting dust, more out of frustration than lack of interest. I greatly admired others who played but had to admit that I did not have a good ear for music.

I liked sports, but my success was reminiscent of my high school basketball days. After four years of being on the team, I received a trophy for "trying the hardest and missing the most baskets." Swimming was my sport of choice, an activity for personal enjoyment where I could include the girls. I liked the exercise without the pressure to perform.

As I was pondering all these choices I had made, I felt this deep longing to master one thing in my life. My career choice, my crocheting, my swimming—I knew none of these was the answer. I did not know what could be so fulfilling to me that I would stick with it for years. I prayed, "I know that I am just thirty-two today, but I feel like a 'jack of all trades and a master of none.'"

I kept pouring out my heart to God. I told Him I wanted to learn to do something that I would absolutely love. Parenting was my greatest desire and joy, but I was longing to learn something else—I did not know what. I told God I did not care if anyone else ever saw it as an accomplishment, but I did need it to be both meaningful and personally rewarding.

Suddenly I knew what I wanted to learn! I rolled off the sofa onto my knees and cried out, "Lord, would you please teach me to pray, that I might *move your hand through prayer.*"

Chapter 3

How to Move God's Hand

WHAT WAS I THINKING? What was I doing asking God to teach me to pray so that I could move His hand? This seemed like an arrogant request. Who did I think I was, asking God to move in response to my prayers?

Then I remembered characters in the Bible who had entreated God and seen His hand move in response. Moses had moved God's hand several times on behalf of the Israelites during their journey between the Red Sea and the Jordan River (Exodus and Numbers). Hannah had moved the hand of God when crying out for a baby (1 Samuel 1). The one hundred and twenty followers of Christ moved the hand of God while praying together in the upper room (Acts 2).

This helped me understand that my request was in line with God's Word. I began to realize that the longing in my heart was probably put there by God.

As I started moving forward in my new quest, I found a crucial element needed in order to pray with results. Without deliberately looking for a key to moving the hand of God, I discovered something that is probably the *most significant thing in this book.*

I realized that the times when my prayers most effectively moved the hand of God were the times when I first *moved His heart.* When my love for the Father is so deep that everything else fades away, the result is an intense passion to be used by Him. It is during these times of intimacy and surrender that I long to know what is on His heart. It is only then that I truly know how to pray.

God responds to my cries when *brokenness* [humility] and a *pure devotion* are the underlying position of my heart towards *Him,* not towards the prayer request. *It is my sincerity of heart that touches His heart, which in turn moves His hand.*

When I was a little girl, I was taught the following bedtime prayer. Some of you may have learned it as well:

Now I lay me down to sleep,
I pray the Lord my soul to keep.
If I should die before I wake,
I pray the Lord my soul to take.[1]

Then I asked God to bless everyone I knew:

God bless Mommy, Daddy,
Jean, Marilyn, and Elaine,

Grandma and Grandpa,
all my aunts, uncles, and cousins,
and all my friends. Amen

For years I prayed this faithfully as soon as I crawled into bed. I felt guilty if I did not say the prayer. It was such a bedtime habit that as I grew older I continued to say it— only this time while I was brushing my teeth. After all, how could I possibly waste sixty seconds of time in bed praying when I could be thinking about boys or the latest fashion?

How do you view prayer? Do you think it is something we must do in order to feel right with God? Is the condition of our heart important? Does it really matter how we connect?

Let's consider the childhood prayer that I recited thousands of times. The last part is good. Speaking blessing over others is vital. However, I think my blessings were a little impersonal as I asked God to bless Jean, Marilyn, and Elaine. Jean and Marilyn are my older sisters—but "Elaine"? I didn't even know God well enough after talking to Him for years to personalize my prayer and ask God to bless *me.*

Let's look at the first part of the prayer. It is also good to ask God to keep (protect) your soul. Your soul is actually your mind, will, and emotions, but I am not sure if that is the poet's intention. The poet's meaning more likely "spirit," sometimes referred to as "soul."

But the Bible says the only way to heaven is to believe that Jesus died on the cross for our sins. (See John 3:16; 14:6; Romans 5.)

I was a little short on understanding when I simply asked God to take me to heaven when I died. And I only asked him to take me if I died in my sleep!

I am still here, so God answered my innocent communication and protected me. There was probably an element of sincerity in my prayers when I was a little girl. However, I do not think that I was touching God's heart much when I was reciting the words while spitting out toothpaste. As adults we often practice the same kind of daily prayer routine and mean it about as much as I did brushing my teeth.

Now that I have a personal relationship with Jesus, I love to pray more than almost anything else I can do with my time. To me, communicating with God is the most incredible privilege. It brings more joy than I could have imagined. Even though prayer can be intense at times, I do not feel prayer is boring or perform it as a duty. Meaningful prayer time is my choice.

So how do we move God's heart? It is our sincerity of heart that touches His heart, which in turn moves His hand.

In the upcoming chapters I would like to share seven personal stories of prayer for everything from rent to terrorism. There are principles that I learned through each experience. By sharing them, I hope to make a difference in your prayer life.

Moving God's Hand for Provision

HERE ARE TIMES IN the life of a single mom that no matter how diligent you are with your finances, circumstances can unexpectedly alter your income. There are so many things in life to consider when a woman is the sole parent and provider that planning far ahead is not always the priority.

When God says in Psalm 68:5 that He is Father to the fatherless, we can be confident that He can arrange for provision in ways not even an earthly father would consider.

One day when my three children were very young, a check I was expecting did not arrive. It was the day the rent was due, and I knew of nothing I could do to alter the situation by the end of the banking day. I desperately needed God's hand to move in the area of finances, so at nine o'clock in the morning, as soon as the two older girls left for school, I began to pray.

This particular day, I prayed hour upon hour in the same way that I would do a day's work hour after hour. I talked to God about the need; I thanked Him for hearing my prayer; I praised Him that He was the Father to the fatherless.

At exactly 4 p.m. the doorbell rang, and there stood a local businessman. He and his wife were friends from the church I attended. He said, "While I have been working today, I had the recurring thought that you were in need. It wouldn't leave me, so I decided to come by and see what it is you require, so maybe I can help."

"Eight hundred dollars for my rent today," I responded. He looked somewhat surprised, but then smiled, knowing God had sent him to my door. Within thirty minutes the rent money was in my bank account.

I have seen God's hand move many times in my life in the area of finances. I must note, however, that the answers to our prayers are so obviously ordained of God that one can never take for granted how God will respond to a need, especially a financial one. He may open the way for you to get more work, show you how to cut expenses, give you a creative idea to stretch what you have, or He may move on someone else's heart to help you.

Each answer is evidence of His great mercy. Each time He is looking at the *heart.*

Principle # 1

You do the praying. Make room for God to answer as He wills.

Chapter 5

Moving God's Hand for Healing

I HAVE OFTEN SAID THAT the best time to pray for a miracle is *before* we need one. The time we spend with God before we get sick helps us to believe the passages in the Bible that refer to healing. (See 1 Peter 2:24; Psalm 107:20; Luke 9:11.) Jesus often withdrew from the crowds to spend time with the Father. Then He walked amongst the people and performed many miracles. (See Luke 5:16–26.)

When we think of healing, we often think of being touched by God concerning a physical ailment in our lives. There are many stories about physical healing in my other books, *A Time to Heal* and *The Story Behind Home with a Heart*, that line up with this thought. However, Jesus spent much of His healing ministry casting out demons.

One evening I was spending time in prayer and reading my Bible, as was my routine. It was getting late, so I prepared to head to bed. Suddenly there was a knock at my door. Surprised because of the late hour, I checked carefully to see who was knocking. There in the dark stood a young woman in her late teens crying uncontrollably. I thought I recognized her so I cautiously opened the door. Through the sobs she blurted out, "Elaine, help me, or I am going to kill myself. I can't take it any more." Startled by her words, I immediately invited her into my home, unaware of any reason for such distress in her life.

She slumped down in a heap on the carpet in the middle of my living room repeating, "Please help me. Please help me."

I knew this young woman was a Christian, but because I had no understanding of her struggle, I had no idea what to do. Nevertheless, I had just been in the presence of God. I inwardly prayed, "I surrender to the Holy Spirit."

I immediately discerned the demonic activity that was holding her in bondage. I spoke with authority: "In the name of Jesus I command…to get out." I named three spirits, one right after the other.

Within a couple minutes she was a different woman. She was still crying, but this time in gratitude to God. Then she calmly shared her story and left my home. Her life was dramatically changed that night and she grew to become a beautiful Christian woman, wife, and mother.

Did it make a difference to the outcome of the evening that

I had been spending time with God when this happened? Of course it did. Otherwise I would never have been able to discern so quickly the reason for this woman's distress, nor would I have been able to move in the same level of authority in prayer.

I truly believe that the best time to pray is before we need the hand of God to move. It was the intimacy with my Father ahead of time that brought my faith to a level to believe for this young woman to be set free.

I am sadly aware that many of us have experienced the loss of a family member or a friend who has been the focus of our prayers for healing. At such times we all have many unanswered questions. We must then acknowledge the painful reality that sometimes our prayers for healing are not answered as we hoped.

I appreciate the wisdom of a very dear man, Pastor Arnold Kalamen, on praying for healing. He once said to me, "As long as there is life, we pray." And I conclude that we continue to trust God.

We want to do whatever we can to see His healing come to ourselves or loved ones. As we spend time in the presence of God, we will walk in a greater anointing to see His hand move for healing.

Principle # 2

Time spent reading the Bible and being in God's presence increases our level of authority over Satan.

Chapter 6

Moving God's Hand for Ministries

*I*F YOU ARE WILLING to allow God to use you in prayer, you may find yourself forerunning events that you may never have dreamed possible.

Pastor Bill Wilson is the founder of Metro Ministries International. The first time I heard him speak, my heart was knit to his passion for abandoned children. The second time I heard him speak, God put it on my heart to ask him to write a foreword for my handbooks to single mothers.

My own pastor had previously told me that someone of great influence would add a foreword to my work. My response was, "I do not know any such person." But two years later, while listening to Pastor Bill tell how his mother had abandoned him on the streets as a boy, I knew he was the man to ask.

Little did I know that this one request to Pastor Bill would lead me to years of commitment to pray for his ministry. What I also did not know then is that God calls us to forerun in prayer what He asks others to do in the natural. God has us working as one body.

Metro Ministries was already a very large ministry in North America when I began to pray. I believe God showed me new things that were to come in the ministry, usually two or three years ahead of time, that would strengthen it here and launch it internationally.

I would write in a journal what I saw was to come, then begin to focus my prayers strategically. Sure enough, a few years later I would hear how the ministry had expanded in that exact area. There were foundational changes, new concepts for expansion into other countries, prayers for the children in these countries, a ranch for sexually exploited children, a training center for leaders in New York, and expansion into television.

Praying is not a glamorous ministry with accolades from man. If you need the approval of man, you will find the call to pray very unfulfilling. But if you are willing to see the kingdom of God expand without personal recognition, then there is absolutely nothing more rewarding.

The only reason I am sharing my stories is to encourage others that their lives can make a huge difference in the kingdom of God, while never having to leave home. Many of us can't go into the front lines of ministry, and that is okay. We can still be a big part of what God is doing in the world.

Praying for financial support for such a large ministry as Metro is an ongoing plea before God. However, there was a very specific prayer request that was prayed in secret, yet God gave me the privilege to know when it was answered.

If any of you are familiar with Pastor Bill's work in under-developed countries, you know that he has put his health at risk many times to reach abandoned kids. One year when physically weakened, he contracted tuberculosis.

I remember that it was early fall. Even though he was very sick, he continued to go from church to church and from one television interview to another to raise the funds needed for the children's Christmas stocking giveaway. While watching television one evening, I saw Pastor Bill sharing with the host and audience. He was very sick, yet desperately trying to communicate the immense need to give Christmas stockings to the 30,000 children who go the Sunday school in Brooklyn.

My heart was moved, but I had nothing to give. As I started to pray, I was surprised to hear myself asking, "Father, please tell Pastor Benny Hinn to give Pastor Bill $100,000 for the Christmas project." It was a simple prayer. I thought nothing more of it as I continued to watch the program. Nevertheless, I must have moved God's heart with my sincerity because two weeks later I saw God's hand move. I was watching *This Is Your Day* with Pastor Benny when he said, "Do you know what? God just told me last night to give Bill Wilson $100,000 for his kids for Christmas."

Now how much more rewarding can prayer get than that!

Many of you may have already partnered with a ministry for prayer. If not, I want to encourage you to do so. Ministries need people supporting them in prayer. God sees what you do in secret and will bless you for your faithfulness in His kingdom. (See Matthew 6:4–18.)

Principle # 3

Do not pray because you want the approval of man. Be willing to see the kingdom of God expand without personal recognition.

Chapter 7

Moving God's Hand for Protection

ODAY I WATCHED THE television coverage of the funeral of Coretta Scott King, widow of civil rights leader Martin Luther King Jr.—shot and killed in 1968. Thankfully his wife carried the torch for his vision in the years since his untimely death. However, his precious life ended far too soon. We must pray protection for our leaders in government and ministries.

Another time since I first committed to praying for Metro Ministries, I stepped into any area of intercession that was completely different from any previously mentioned but even more vital.

It was Sunday, March 2, 2003, as I sat at the dinner table to eat when I clearly heard God speak to me. He told me to enter into a strict time of fasting and prayer for the next three days and not to work during this time. Often I had fasted and prayed, but never before did I know so emphatically that I was to lay everything down, even my work.

The next day was the World Day of Prayer, so I presumed this was the reason. But as Monday ended and the prayer for the nations left my heart, I still was terribly burdened. I prayed throughout the evening and continued in prayer the next day.

When you have such an urgency to pray, but do not know why you are praying, the only thing you can do is to keep yielding to the Holy Spirit. I understood that it was a serious issue if I was not to be working, yet after two days I still had little understanding of what this prayer time was about. By Tuesday evening I knew there was danger ahead for someone. A while later I realized it was Pastor Bill's life that was at risk. This insight provided more clarity on how to pray.

Fasting doesn't move God's hand; it just helps our flesh to get out of the way, humbling us to be more sensitive to what the Holy Spirit is doing. Tuesday evening there was a prayer meeting for *Home with a Heart*, which is the homemaking program I wrote for single mothers. The ladies who attend know me very well and trust me. I brought up my concern and we prayed together. After a few hours of sleep Tuesday night, I was up and in prayer again. It was now Wednesday, March 5th.

That afternoon I had a doctor's appointment. While driving to the clinic, which is in the lovely little town of Niagara-on-the-Lake, Ontario, I became distracted by all the scenery and quaintness of the old town. When I arrived home, I realized that even that short detour from prayer was wrong. It wasn't the appointment that was wrong, but losing focus while going. I asked God's forgiveness. This was not a time to be negligent in what I was to be doing. I went back into prayer.

At that time I attended a weekly Bible study on Wednesday evenings. I thought maybe I should still go and ask others to join me in prayer again. Once there I changed my mind. The gathering was very social, the atmosphere light. It seemed like the wrong time to bring up the matter on my heart.

By 9 p.m. I felt restless, almost anxious inside. I have learned to appreciate that this happens when the Holy Spirit is nudging me. Since we were finished with the study, I decided to go home to pray alone. The minute I stepped out of the door from the study, I started into intercession for Pastor Bill once more. At 9:30 p.m. I was again kneeling at my bedside, praying for his protection so intensely that I felt like I was in the middle of whatever was happening. I continued for several hours into the night, then went to sleep.

My phone ringer had been off for three days. Thursday morning I decided to check my messages. There was one from my pastor, "Elaine, did you hear about Pastor Bill? He has been shot! Call me."

Those of you who are acquainted with Metro Ministries already know that at 9:30 p.m., Wednesday March 5, 2003, Pastor Bill was shot in the face. Two men robbed him at gunpoint near the Brooklyn Bridge. One of the robbers shoved a revolver into the roof of his mouth and fired, but the round did not go off. Realizing what had just happened, he fought the man with the gun, pulling him to the ground. The second shot tore through the side of his face, miraculously missing the bones. In a semiconscious state with severe bleeding, Pastor Bill drove himself to the hospital. A medical team then saved his life.

Is being obedient in prayer a matter of life and death? Indeed it is. My obedience during the three-day preparation was key to being sensitive to the Holy Spirit at the exact time of the shooting and the crucial hours that followed. Those timely prayers may have blocked that first bullet, which he may not have survived.

In the book of Esther in the Bible, her fasting and prayers saved the lives of the whole nation of Jewish people. (See Esther 5–9.)

I repeat; we must be faithful to pray for those in authority.

Principle # 4

When you have an urgency to pray, yet do not know to what it pertains, keep yielding to the Holy Spirit.

Chapter 8

Moving God's Hand for Political Leaders

I HAVE FOUND OVER MY years of prayer that when God calls you to a season of prayer, you must be willing to carry the burden without the help of others. Sometimes you can rally a team of people who may have the same interest, but more times than not, you carry it alone.

This is not a bad thing. It is just a reality. Since I had asked God to teach me how to pray, I should not expect that others would necessarily be interested too. But early on in my prayer journey I used to think that everyone would be as excited as me to pray about certain things.

This happened with a Canadian election just two years after my request to be used in prayer. The 1984 federal election was my first large undertaking to move the hand of God.

While watching the national Progressive Conservative leadership convention when Joe Clark was elected a few years earlier, I had the impression that Brian Mulroney was to be the next Conservative Prime Minister of Canada.

When the election was announced, I was called to prayer. There had been occasions in the past when I had done some campaigning for federal elections, but I was not fervent in the political arena.

This time I was very passionate. I took on the burden to win this election. I worked as hard for the Progressive Conservative Party in prayer as I think anyone must have worked on the campaign trail. Interestingly, I never was able to solicit anyone else to join me. When I would enthusiastically bring it up at a prayer group, my idea was met with indifference and, "Anything else?"

Nevertheless, I loved every minute of this secret adventure. The day of the election finally arrived and I was glued to the television for the results. My little girls thought this was great fun; it was like a party to them. We were eating lots of fun foods and in front of the TV, even—a rare event in our home! Amy was nine years old and she had some understanding of what all the excitement was about. Sure enough as votes were tallied, the Progressive Conservatives won one riding after another across the country. In fact they won the largest majority government in Canadian history, taking 211 out of the 282 seats. Brian Mulroney was the new Prime Minister.

In my little house far away from Ottawa, my daughters and I were celebrating and hollering just as much as the delegates on Parliament Hill and in the individual ridings. The only difference was the fizzle in our drinks was from Sprite, not champagne. I couldn't have been happier if I had been in the midst of the festive celebrations. And no one, until this day, even knew that I took part in the election.

Principle # 5

When God calls you to a season of prayer, you must be willing to carry the burden without the help of others.

Chapter 9

Moving God's Hand for Our Land

As a single mother, I am very protective of my Friday evening hours. I am often tired, therefore more vulnerable, so I choose carefully what I do with my time. I would like to go back to another date in time to show how our choices can affect the lives of others. It was Friday evening, July 26, 1996. At nine o'clock my thoughts were reviewing the past week's work, and I was deciding what I would do for a few hours of relaxation. Without seriously thinking about it, I began to talk to God about what was on His heart.

Suddenly I stopped deciding and began to pray. The intensity of the prayer soon made me realize that something terrible was about to happen. I could hear people's screams of terror in my spirit. Then the words "terrorism is upon the land" kept coming to me repeatedly.

I continued to pray against terrorism as I thought God was leading me. I had no idea what was taking place in the natural. I prayed for three or more hours then went to bed.

The next morning I turned the TV on to CNN. Just after 1 a.m. July 27, a bomb exploded at Centennial Park in Atlanta, Georgia, during the summer Olympic Games. One woman died and 111 people were injured.[1]

Did my prayers protect some people's lives? I do not know for sure, but I trust they did. Once again I was obedient to pray. I was saddened, but not surprised to hear the news of the bombing the next morning.

From the years 1994 through 1998, I prayed against terrorism toward the World Trade Center. It was not something on my mind until one day when I was traveling in New York City near the twin towers. While looking in a bookstore, I felt God directed me to buy a topographical map of the city. When I opened it and saw the twin towers, I believe God put it on my heart to start to pray against terrorism specific to the towers.

I had not thought much about the earlier acts of terrorism in 1993 against the towers until I began to pray against terrorism. I had known about the attacks, but that news had little impact on my life. I was Canadian, living in beautiful British Columbia—about as far from New York City as you can get in North America—absorbed with raising my girls. I truly didn't feel the implications of the terrorism as it pertains to the world today. As a reminder of what took place, here is a quote from Wikipedia.

> In the World Trade Center bombing (February 26, 1993) a car bomb was detonated by Arab Islamist terrorists in the underground parking garage below Tower One of the World Trade Center in New York City. The 1,500-lb (680 kg) urea nitrate-fuel oil device killed six and injured 1,042 people. It was intended to devastate the foundation of the North Tower, causing it to collapse onto its twin.[2]

When God speaks clearly to you to do something, it does not matter if you understand any of the details. The question is: "Do you love Him and His people enough to respond?"

I faithfully prayed daily against terrorist acts destroying the towers for nearly five years. Then I stopped! I am not sure why. There was much focus on family events in my life during that specific year. My two elder daughters married. At Christmas between the two summer weddings, my mom died. I was close to her and needed time to grieve. Two other family members died within a year. I never thought about the World Trade Center in prayer again—until that fateful day when two hijacked planes flew into the towers.

Everyone remembers where they were on September 11, 2001. I was sitting in front of the TV watching the news that morning as it happened. I stared in utter disbelief, as so many of you did. But having been so intimately connected with the whole thing previously in prayer, I fell face downward in despairing grief.

For days I agonized, feeling responsible for every single death. Why had I stopped praying? What did I do wrong? Many were grieving the loss of a loved one. I was grieving the loss of everyone who died. No one will ever understand what I went through. I could hardly bear my anguish, let alone explain it to anyone.

However, God became my comfort, as He did for us all. I can only hope that God lifted the prayer burden from me the year when the needs of my family grew. Whatever the answer is to this, I know that He loves me. He is a loving Father.

Principle # 6

When God speaks clearly to you to pray, it does not matter if you understand any details. The question is: "Do you love Him and His people enough to respond?"

Chapter 10

Moving God's Hand for Families

EACH OF US HAS a place of authority in society that is uniquely different from that of someone else. The police carry authority in the area of law, yet would not have the same impact on society if they were preaching a Sunday morning sermon. A music teacher has authority in her classroom; but if she walked into the art room to teach a topic that was not her specialty, she would not have the same authority with the art students as she does in her own classroom.

So it is in our own homes where we carry authority. For example, I can parent my children in the way that I feel is correct and I carry the authority to do so. However, I do not have the right to walk into my neighbor's home and tell her children what to do.

I have very clearly seen the importance of staying in your area of authority in connection to my work with single moms. If a mom comes into the *Home with a Heart* program, I influence her to manage her home more effectively. It is a place of authority that God has given to me.

I am using these examples to explain that, as mothers, we carry great authority in our own homes in prayer. Titus 2:4–5 (KJV) tells us that we are to be keepers of the home. That certainly refers to homemaking, but we also need to be keepers of the home spiritually, especially if there is no husband to do so.

Over the years I have found my times with God to be invaluable to help me see His heart for what can affect our homes with wrong spiritual influences. Every year the influences get worse. There is a ten-year age difference between my youngest daughter, Laura, and her sister Natalie. I look back at the spiritual protection that was needed to guard over my older girls compared to what it takes now to pray for my youngest, and I see far more doors of evil that could potentially harm Laura. God has a good plan for our children, while Satan has a plan to abort it.

I cannot change what the media is presenting, even though I speak out when I can, but I can carry authority in my home as to what comes in through TV, magazines, music, and Internet.

I love what one friend said to me years ago. She was sitting and watching a movie. Suddenly the thought was impressed upon her, which she believes was from the Lord: "Do not be entertained by anything that Jesus died for." That is a profound thought. If we all lived by that principle, we wouldn't watch many movies, would we?

We all want the leaders of our nation to change our country so it is a better place for us to live. Our country will change when we, as individuals, take the responsibility to live godly lives and train our children to do likewise. That responsibility is ours in our own homes, whether we are the president or a single mother.

We must humble ourselves and pray. There is no other answer to heal our homes, and thus our nation, from our enemies of drugs, alcohol, abuse, immorality, abortion, violence, materialism, and terrorism. (See 2 Chronicles 7:14.) Praying for our families is our first privilege.

We are in a war for our children. The enemy is not taking time off from luring our children, so we cannot afford to take time off from praying for them. Pray as though you are a soldier in a war, not a lady in distress. We must take up the need with earnestness. In a military war, specific plans are drawn for battle.

Since all of our children are different, we must ask God for strategy in prayer for each one. With it is the realization that Satan cunningly seeks to deceive our children through his lies.

Just look at how the media influences our children. Media bombards our homes with disrespect for authority, sexual immorality, occultism, violence, idolatry, and so much more that opposes the Word of God. It makes evil look good and good look evil. In fact, it makes "good" look downright stupid. We must guard our children by pushing back the lies until they see truth for themselves. Satan is known as "the father of liars" (John 8:44). Take your authority, in Jesus' name, against lying and deceiving spirits.

Many of our children suffer from the wounds of abandonment or abuse, the horrible effects of today's violence, or the occult. I exhort you, *take up your place of prayer over your children.* If they are young, you can lay your hands on them and pray when they are sleeping. Ask God to heal their hurts and command that any demonic strongholds that your child may have knowingly or unknowingly given place to leave him or her. As they get older, use every opportunity for prayer, whether you are doing the laundry or shutting yourself away in your prayer closet.

To be effective you must first rid yourself of any fear, for you have all authority over the enemy. "The earnest prayer of a righteous man has great power and wonderful results" (James 5:16).

Contend until you have won your children for Christ, and then continue praying even when they leave the nest and marry. Guard over their marriages and the next generation to come. The reward is worth the effort. But keep in mind the most important message of this book: you will move God's hand for your family by remembering to *first move His heart.*

Principle #7

Pray as though you are a soldier in a war, not a lady in distress. Push back the darkness for others until they see truth for themselves.

Chapter 11

You Are the Answer to Your Own Prayers

ONE EVENING I WAS washing the dinner dishes and thinking about getting my youngest to bed. It was a time when I least expected to hear God speak. "You are the answer to your own prayers," quietly interrupted the usual clean-up routine.

I did not know what God meant that day. But in looking back and considering what is yet to come, I can see that I am, indeed, an answer to my own prayers—my prayers to strengthen the single-parent home.

How many times have we been concerned about someone or something and, sure enough, we step right into that need? When we do that, we become an answer to our own prayers.

Have you ever felt compassion for a lonely neighbor and then invited her for dinner? Did you ever pray about an anti-abortion issue, then vote for the political leader who stood for life? Were you ever concerned for the future of our children, and became a Sunday school teacher? If so, you were an answer to your own prayers.

The burden that someone carries is key to his or her life's mission. It may be helping a neighbor; it may be helping a nation. I often hear women say that they do not know what to do with their lives, what is their purpose? I certainly advocate that a women's first purpose is mothering if she has children.

Besides that, look around and see what else you really care about. What upsets you? In what area do you want to see change? I get upset when mothers lose their children to foster families because they cannot or will not look after their children. I am thankful that there are safe and healthy choices for these children. More good homes are needed for placement because some children are abused within the system. And that really, really upsets me. I can't imagine how abusers get licensed.

But what deeply grieves me is that many of these moms have no role models to prevent them from losing their children in the first place. Many women have come from homes of abuse, violence, and drugs and are trying to parent out of their own pain and dysfunction. We need godly women to teach them how to be mothers. We need strong families that can surround a fatherless home with love and direction until that family is strong. Then the authorities wouldn't need to take the children from their mothers. Separation is traumatic for children, regardless of how horrible the home is for them. Often these children are forced to go from one home to another.

Therefore, I am trying to do something about it. I am trying to encourage churches to set up Homemaking Schools to teach moms how to look after their children and homes. Moms can teach themselves with my program as well.

Maybe you are reading this little book and you are a mom needing help. Please reach out and ask someone. Tell them you do not have the skills you need to cope right now. You won't be judged; you will be helped. Many circumstances have caused your situation to be what it is presently. If you do not have a church affiliation, then call The Salvation Army or a pro-life pregnancy center to find the help you need. You can always be redirected to someone near you.

Now that I have poured out what concerns me, what is your burden? Can you start to fill the need for what God has placed on your heart? Take a step of faith and begin to do something in that area. Start with prayer first and then ask God for wisdom and direction. But don't just pray. Look around to see what you can do. Being the answer to your own prayers can be a daily lifestyle; it does not have to be a lifetime mission.

Have you been concerned for a friend? Maybe you can look after her child to lighten her load for a week or two. Perhaps you can phone to encourage someone that keeps coming to your mind. What about giving finances to a ministry that carries the same burden as you? Offering financial assistance is as necessary to a ministry as the people doing the physical work. Possibly you can enter a line of work that directly influences the very area you want to affect.

Whatever your concern, God can use it to touch another life. Watch for these moments; they can pass by quickly.

Many times you will find *you are the answer to your own prayers*.

Chapter 12

The Dance of Deception

I WISH TO GIVE THIS caution to single mothers: make sure that your prayer burden is in line with the Bible. Specifically if you are praying for an individual of the opposite sex, be cautious about your motive. A weak-willed woman may be swept into deception because she is praying for something that originated in her soul instead from the Holy Spirit. For clearer understanding on the difference between the spirit and soul, please read *A Time to Heal*.[1]

Are you on a mission to pray for a man, believing the prayer burden you carry is from the Lord, when in fact your motive is to have a personal relationship with the man? To be certain, test the spirit. If this man is your husband, it most likely is a God-given call to prayer. However, connecting yourself in prayer to a man for whom you feel an emotional attraction can be devastating if it is not God's plan for you.

Examine the fruit in your own life as you commit to pray

for a man with whom you have an excessive affection, whether through personal contact or developed in prayer. Does the commitment bring joy, peace, self-control, and more fruit of the Holy Spirit, or is it driving you to unhealthy behavior, confusion, obsession, and disruption in your home? Does it overrule your common sense? A commitment that is not from God will hurt you in the end and, worse yet, your children.

A woman can easily fall into this trap through her natural desire to have a partner or even to carry out a mission of rescue. The deception may also come from a word that she thought was from God, but instead was her own voice, a deceiving spirit, or possibly even a false prophecy. Never put a voice above the Bible's truths.

A few years ago I received a call from a single mom as a result of her seeing me on *Living the Life*, a television show produced by CBN. She was purchasing the *Home with a Heart* program, and wanted me to bring a seminar to her area. I felt it was right, so we started planning the event. As I was getting to know this gal, I became involved in helping her personally. I love to mentor, but I can help only a few women at any given time. It would be a wonderful contribution to our society if every woman would take at least one younger woman under her wing.

As we were working on seminar details, it became evident that this mother was having difficulty managing her home. We put aside the seminar in order to focus on her personal parenting and homemaking skills. It was not long into the process when I discovered the reason she was so unfocused at home. Her time, energy, and prayers were misdirected towards "saving" a relationship with a man in her life, rather than into how to better nurture the little girls for whom she was responsible. The fruit in her home was confusion and frustration, which were preventing her from functioning effectively as a mother.

Later I found a poem that addresses this problem exactly:

The Dance of Deception

The Dance of Deception...began to play
the moment I started walking your way.
It's the Dance of Deception...
Won't you join me, my dear;
as I softly lie all you've wanted to hear.
I possess all you've ever wanted to see
but remember, my darling...it's just fantasy.

So...You would like to dance...
Let our dance begin
as I stoke the fire of passion within.
My lie is your truth
and my love you believe;
But remember, my darling,
I've come to deceive.

Let us dance through the night
and the rest of our days...
You see, my heart is True

it's yours that Betrays!
You believed my lie
that was truly spoken
The Dance of Deception…
is a Promise to be Broken![2]

—Allison McPeak

I need to stress to you that it is extremely important to guard your heart and watch your motive in prayer. Be sure to stay balanced in your prayer life by reading the Word and seeking godly counsel if necessary.

Be accountable to strong Christian women if you feel confused in an area of prayer. Do not seek out only one counselor, as she may be deceived or have hidden sin in her life. There is safety in having more than one counselor in this area.

Jesus says, "For My yoke is easy and My burden is light" (Matt. 11:30, NKJV). Prayer should not weigh us down or bring anxiety. When the moment of prayer is over, we should be free to carry on our day without heaviness.

It is important to note that trying to control someone or their choices is manipulation, which can be a weapon of spiritual witchcraft. Keep your motives pure in prayer. Man has a free will. Our only goal is to keep the darkness away from those for whom God has truly called us to pray. We are to speak blessing over them, not determine what God's plans are for their lives. Be careful!

We are merely vehicles through whom the Holy Spirit can direct prayers. Be sure that you do not dance with deception in your desire to see someone change. Remember, your intimacy with God and accountability to others are key to discernment in prayer.

Chapter 13

Learning to Pray Effectively

So HOW CAN WE learn to pray effectively and not be deceived? I suppose there are as many ways to pray as there are people who pray. Since each of us is unique, so is our prayer relationship with our Father in heaven.

However, Jesus did set an example for us to follow with the Lord's Prayer. Let us look at it closely to see how it can help protect us from the lies of the enemy.

By beginning my prayer times with this example, I know I am in the will of God. Then I can safely enter into the next stage of prayer: asking God to show me anything on His heart about which He would specifically have me pray. I will explain how my prayer time develops so you can see why I trust His voice to lead me.

I have used a version of the Bible that many of us memorized as children. Then I put it in my own words, as I do in prayer, to make it more intimate and personal. The meaning of each sentence is powerful as you carefully ponder it. The Lord's prayer is found in Matthew 6:9–13:

> Our Father in heaven, Hallowed be Your name.

Hallowed simply means "honored". I begin my prayer times by honoring God for who He is. This is praise. You can honor Him with your words, by singing, by reading the Psalms, or listening to music; whatever kind of praise is comfortable for you.

> Your kingdom come. Your will be done on earth as it is in heaven.

This is a time of surrender. I surrender my will, desires, thoughts, imaginations, and burdens. I let everything go and tell God that I only want His will. This leads me into worship, which is a greater adoration than praise. As I set my eyes on the Lord, my thoughts move away from work, my children, and the broken vacuum. This is not as easy as it sounds. If I do not get my agenda out of the way and really mean that I do want to see His kingdom come, then I probably will not see it.

> Give us this day our daily bread.

I thank God for His provision. If there is a personal need, this is the time to ask for God's help.

And forgive us our debts, as we forgive our debtors.

In this context, *debt* means "sin." Any sin in my life that I have not confessed can hinder the answer to my prayers. I ask God to forgive my sins and I forgive anyone who has sinned against me. Again, it sounds easy. Many unanswered prayers stem from this one sin of being unable to forgive.

And do not lead us into temptation, but deliver us from the evil one.

At this time I ask God to keep me from being deceived or being tempted to sin. I pray for His protection for my children, family, and friends. James 4:7 reads, "Resist the devil and he will flee." I resist any attack of Satan against my family or against my prayer time in Jesus' name.

For Yours is the kingdom and the power and the glory forever. Amen.

I give all glory to God. It is about Him, not me. Then I proceed to seek God's heart for the rest of my prayer time. He reveals this to me through His Word, an impression of someone or some place, or occasionally a vision. God speaks to us quietly from deep within. It is a "knowing" inside. Again, if you have hidden sin or wrong motives, you may not discern correctly. Keep yourself humble before the Lord. (See 1 Peter 5:5–6.)

By the time I have gone through the Lord's Prayer, intimacy with God has developed and it is easier to know what He is communicating about further prayer. It's the same as in any relationship. The more time you spend communicating with a person, the deeper the intimacy. The deeper the intimacy, the more you can know a person's thoughts.

I pray about what God has shown me for as long as my prayer time lasts, or until He impresses me with something else to do or pray. If God wants to reveal something to me about my own life, it is usually at this time of surrender, after I have put aside my own thoughts and agenda. It is often difficult to pray for ourselves and those dearest to us without being emotionally involved, so it does take determination to lay down our will in order to pray effectively for personal issues.

I often say in prayer, "Give me Your heart, Father." I find that as God gives me His heart for others and I am faithful to pray, many times needs in my own life are met. The important point about praying is simply doing it. Be yourself with God; communication and intimacy will develop naturally.

As you can see by some of my examples in previous chapters, each prayer time is different and, for sure, never boring. Once again, the key to knowing what to do is to keep yielding to the Holy Spirit. If you read through one of the Gospels you will see Jesus prayed for people as the Father led Him, and each time it was different.

Remember, the *sincerity of your heart touches His heart, which in turn moves His hand.*

Chapter 14

Methods of Prayer

WHEN I FIRST BEGAN to pray, I did not realize that God was teaching me how to pray different kinds of prayers. I now know that prayer can come in many forms—prayers of praise and worship, prayers of thanksgiving, prayers of declaration, prayers of petition (on your own behalf), and prayers of intercession (on behalf of someone else). Most of these forms of prayer are in the Lord's Prayer.

The Bible has many examples of different methods of prayer. I personally spend the most time on intercession. My favorite scriptures on intercession are in the book of Esther, who interceded on behalf of the Jewish people. Psalm 103 is my favorite worship passage, and I love Psalm 121 for declaring who God is.

This Psalm became my strength when my youngest daughter, Laura, was born. I was having my baby alone after only ten months in a second marriage. She was born three months after the separation and I was lacking in prenatal preparation.

My focus was on making a new home for my children, nothing else. There were complications with my first two pregnancies that resulted in twenty hours of labor with each baby. I was hoping this delivery would be different but was realistic enough to know that I could be in for a difficult labor again. I had an extra concern for this little one's safe arrival because she had been a twin. I lost the other baby traumatically earlier in the pregnancy. Far away from family and friends, I knew that only the Word of God would pull me through.

I arrived at the hospital at six o'clock on a Wednesday evening in March and recited Psalm 121 over and over until ten after two the following afternoon. The nurses kept requesting that I call someone to be with me at the hospital, but I knew what I required to deliver this baby. As great as a support person may have been through labor, I needed more. There was no doubt in my mind that to see me through, I needed to be focused on God and declaring who He is.

When the doctor and nurses started more intense monitoring and whispering at one o'clock in the morning about the loss of a heartbeat and further complications, I declared with even more faith, "I will lift up mine eyes unto the hills, from whence cometh my help. My help cometh from the

Lord, which made heaven and earth," well memorized from the King James Version.

My beautiful, perfectly healthy baby girl was born that Thursday afternoon. I have often wondered how many times I declared this verse in more than twenty hours of labor, but the important thing to note is the *power in declaration.* I was weary at her birth, but not strained. By noon the next day I was taking my third little girl home.

Is it not incredible that the Creator of everything in heaven and earth is available for us to talk to any minute of any day, in many different ways? And that day in the hospital it truly was every minute that I spoke to Him.

Think of some of the miraculous Bible stories. We actually communicate with the same God who parted the Red Sea so His children could be freed from Egyptian bondage, sent an angel to shut the mouths of the lions to protect Daniel in the den, caused Jonah to live in a whale's belly until he obeyed Him. (See Exodus 13–14; Daniel 6; Jonah 1–2.)

There is not one thing we cannot talk to God about— our children's needs, our own hurts, our many decisions, birthing babies, and whom He wants to run the country.

Chapter 15

Don't Give Up

MANY OF US HAVE heard it said that successful people are persistent people. God also refers to persistence in the Bible in reference to having our prayers answered. One of my favorite Bible passages about prayer is the story of the widow.

"There was a city judge," he said, "a very godless man who had great contempt for everyone. A widow of that city came to him frequently to appeal for justice against a man who had harmed her. The judge ignored her for a while, but eventually she got on his nerves.

"'I fear neither God nor man,' he said to himself, 'but this woman bothers me. I'm going to see that she gets justice, for she is wearing me out with her constant coming!'"

Then the Lord said, "If even an evil judge can be worn down like that, don't you think that God will surely give justice to his people who plead with him day and night? Yes! He will answer them quickly! But the question is: When I, the Messiah, return, how many will I find who have faith [and are praying]?"

—Luke 18:2–8

We would all see more answers to prayer if we followed the widow's example of persistence. I wonder how many of us have given up praying for a desire of our heart—just before the prayer was answered. We grow weary or discouraged and think there is no point in continuing to pray.

Think of prayer like a project or job in the natural. If we are not accustomed to working until a job is completed, we will most likely not be able to pray until the answer comes.

God revealed something one day about why some of our prayers seem to take so long to be answered. We pray inconsistently. We see a need for which we want to pray. When we see a partial answer to our prayers, even though the complete answer has not arrived, we slack off and either stop praying or start praying for something else. Satan then sets up a strategy to thwart or delay the answer to that first prayer. We do not realize it because we are off on another prayer mission or, more detrimentally, just relaxing.

A runner in a race knows to keep his eye on the finish line until he or she reaches it. Slowing down or turning to see what the opponent is doing simply gives the opponent the edge to get ahead. The more I stay persistently focused on one prayer until the answer comes, no matter how many weeks, months, or years it takes, the more finish lines I cross.

I may be praying for two or three topics at one time, such as a person, a government situation, and a ministry. However, I do not jump from ministry to ministry or person to person. Many times I have seen a life changed by keeping one person before the throne of God for several months straight with my undivided focus in prayer. I believe knowing who or what God wants you to pray for is extremely important.

There was a time before I learned to really listen to God's heart that I was spending a lot of time praying for a particular person who was hardened towards the Lord. After several months I told God that I knew the Bible said that He was not willing that any should miss eternal life, but that He knew this person's heart and what it was going to take for it to change. (See 2 Peter 3:9.)

Therefore, I asked God if there was another life that I should focus on in prayer. He sees what seeds may bring forth a harvest now. I then felt to pray for a group of young people who met at my home weekly for Young Life Club. Less than two months later, nine of the youth accepted Christ. The first person I was praying for accepted Christ eighteen years later, after I prayed only a short season in that year. It is important to discern in what area to be persistent.

God's ways are not our ways; His thoughts are so much higher than our thoughts. (See Isaiah 55:8.) I am continually humbled by how different God's answers are from men's. Be persistently seeking His ways.

Prayers are often answered in stages, so be thankful to

God for each step to the ultimate answer you are seeking. Sometimes we are so focused on the final answer that we miss all the smaller miracles on the way. In my first book, *The Story Behind Home with a Heart*, I talked about recounting the miracles of God.[1] I said that it was interesting to find that the more thankful I am, the more blessings there are to recount.

Do you like to give gifts to an ungrateful, whiney person? Do you think God does?

Most prayer is done in secret. No one but God knows what you are doing. This can be compared to the first stages of pregnancy when no one knows you are carrying a baby. Likewise, prayer can be similar to the last stages of pregnancy. You carry the baby so long that you begin to wonder if it will ever be born. The birthing of a long-awaited answer to prayer is the same. Do not give up in prayer before the answer comes.

Bringing a prayer request forward so others can join you is only beneficial if God has directed it. The prayer of agreement is very powerful. (See Matthew 18:19.) However, many times the initial burden gets lost—sometimes to gossip or indifference—as you expect others to help you with what God has put on your heart to do. Be sensitive when and with whom you share your prayer requests.

The writing of *Home with a Heart* was as much a work in prayer as it was putting the words on paper. Beforehand there were years of prayer regarding God healing hurting women and children, my girls and myself included. It took six and a half years to write and publish my first set of handbooks.

One reason why the writing required so much prayer was to protect the manuscript from being lost. When I began the first book I knew very little about computers, so a friend was helping me input the manuscript into the computer. I told him that I had heard some nightmarish stories of people losing their work. He assured me all precautions had been taken—it would not happen to me. Computers were his business.

Guess what? It did happen. But so my dear friend does not feel badly, it was just the beginning of losses. It happened with several other computers along the way also. Books have been lost from the hard drive and lost from CDs. I lost the whole manuscript and all backup CDs when my luggage went missing while traveling, had an editor lose all my formatting, and even had a publishing house lose all my manuscripts.

My family could not understand why it took so much time and money to write and publish books. In my case it was because they kept getting lost. Why would I need to pray? "The thief does not come except to kill, and to steal, and to destroy" (John 10:10, NKJV). Had I not persisted in prayer, or not persisted in rewriting, the work would never have been completed.

Many times I see the answers to my prayers. Sometimes

I do not. I am well aware that I may not see some of the answers in my lifetime. Nevertheless, I have the satisfaction of knowing I have been obedient to God by persisting in prayer until He shows me something else for which to pray.

Hopefully these thoughts on persistence will help you stay focused in an area of prayer. When focusing on being persistent in prayer for others, I often think, "How would I want someone to pray for me, if I were in this situation?" Then I try to pray with the same diligence.

Chapter 16

No Pressure, Please

AVE YOU EVER FELT frustrated as a single mom like I have because you wanted to attend ministry gatherings, and just could not do so without upsetting the whole family? When this first happened to me, I was so disappointed. I was hungry to learn more about God. When the girls were young I longed to hear the guest speakers who were visiting my church or another local assembly with special weekday services.

Most of the time it was so difficult to get to those meetings. I was without a car and I could not afford sitters, but more importantly, I did not believe in leaving the children with babysitters often. The meetings were usually too late for small children to attend. If the girls did go, I usually paid a dear price, as they would be over-tired and cranky the next day.

God spoke something very important to me during those years of raising little ones that has benefited me ever since.

He saw the hunger in my heart and said, "If you are willing to spend the time with Me, I will teach you what you are longing to learn." I trusted God to do just what He said He would do. Over the years God has been faithful to teach me through His Word and through prayer. Consequently, I never feel I missed out by being home with my children.

Maybe it is not you that is originating the pressure to attend extra church functions, but the expectations of others—who believe you should be at church every time the doors open. The passage in Isaiah 40:11 refers to the Lord as a shepherd and it says that "He will gently lead those who are with young" (NKJV). I think this is a beautiful picture of how tenderly He cares for us as mothers with young children.

When my third daughter, Laura, was born, I had a few more opportunities to go to hear speakers. Amy and Natalie were adolescents and could stay up later. Laura loved to sleep in my arms, so for years I could take her to evening services and she would sleep through the whole meeting.

Yet I know that most kids become wide-awake with all the noise and excitement of a group of people. This was the case with my second daughter. Sometimes at weeklong church conferences I see mothers dragging exhausted, crying children out of nurseries late at night. An occasional late night may not affect a child, but a disrupted routine night after night is hard on a little one.

Moms, if you want to attend an evening meeting, may I suggest you let your child have a rest or sleep before the service or even during the service. Some children can fall asleep anywhere if they know it *really* is bedtime. Take their favorite pillow, blanket, and stuffed toy along to reinforce the bedtime routine—even though the location is different.

On the other hand, if you need to stay home with your very young children, do not feel guilty or left out. I do encourage you to spend that time with the Lord, though, and He will teach you at home. God understands your responsibility to your children.

In looking back, I can see that God honored my commitment to my family. My desire to attend meetings to learn more of Him may have seemed more godly, but even good things can throw off our priorities.

With the pressure lifted, I could, and still do, learn what I desire to learn when I need to be at home. Moms, let's put our time in our homes to good use for the kingdom of God, yet not neglect our other responsibilities.

Chapter 17

Seeing Your Children Pray

THE MOST WONDERFUL REWARD to my prayer life is the fruit in my own home. There are now four of us who pray—Amy, Natalie, Laura, and myself. The older girls are now married and in ministry. For many years I was privileged to see my girls enjoy praying while they still lived at home.

Although I have always had a short daily prayer time with my girls, I never made my children pray. Just because I love to pray, I did not expect the girls to love it also. However, once again I realize that example is the best teacher.

When Amy and Natalie, who are now pastors, were in their early teens and leaders of a youth group, they arose at five o'clock every morning to go to the church and pray with the youth pastor. During that same time, Amy was also the youth worship leader. She made prayer the foundation of the team at Monday evening practice. Amy played keyboard and Natalie sang, but prayer was first for them and anyone else who wanted to be a part of the team.

When she was a teenager, Natalie often received calls at home from friends going through struggles. She would mentor them on the phone, and then off she would go to her bedroom to pray for them. To this day Natalie cares immensely for young people. She has either volunteered or been employed as a youth pastor and young adults' pastor since she graduated from Bible school. She became an answer to her own prayers. In fact, both girls have. Amy always carried a burden for discipleship within the church so the members would become strong. Among many other duties that are more administrative, she oversees the women's ministry in her church.

When Laura was a little girl, I saw her prayers move the hand of God. I remember one occasion when she was only four years old; I walked into my room and found her kneeling by my bed. It is an antique bed, so it was a bit of a reach for a little tyke. She did not realize I had entered the room. Laura was earnestly calling out for God's protection for her older sisters, who were traveling with the youth group to a worship conference. She then continued in prayer for nearly half an hour longer making another particular request known to God. Few adults could probably stay focused that long.

Just recently Laura and I were talking during lunch. She had graduated from high school and was unsettled with career choices. She was telling me her thoughts for further education and interim work.

Then just to keep the conversation going, I told her that I was writing another book. She asked what it was about. When I told her that the topic was prayer, she replied, "Mom you may not think that I pray any more, but I want you to know that I still pray a lot. I pray every day when I am driving and every night when I go to bed." To tell you the truth, I was more relieved to hear the fact that she prays in the car more than in bed. I have had enough dings in my car to substantiate the need for prayer there!

As mothers, we have the greatest influence on our children. Let's try to set an example of prayer for them to follow. Start praying for personal needs in the home and allow them to see the answers to small requests in order to build trust in God.

When Amy was in grade nine, she was invited to go skiing with her girlfriend's family. This sport was always out of my budget and not possible for Amy to finance with her small part-time job. However, she prayed about going and little by little we saw all the things she needed come to her—gloves, mask, and money to rent skis. Then just before she was to leave for her fun day on the slopes, she came to me and said, "Mom, do you think I could ask God for a film for my camera?" Obviously, this was before digital!

I said I had no idea if the answer would come on such short notice, but I encouraged her to go ahead. My girls did not have a father in the home, so I had taught them to talk to God as a father. But just as an earthly father does not always provide everything we want, neither does God. Even I was amazed at what happened next.

Her girlfriend Sharleen rang the doorbell less than fifteen minutes after the prayer. Excitedly she said to Amy, "My Dad and I just stopped to buy some film for our camera. The store had a two-for-one sale. Do you want a film for *your* camera?"

I think God was touched by the *sincerity* of Amy's heart. She did not ask out of greed, but humility.

We can have a very positive effect on our children when we pray in the home. Then when they pray, they learn to build their own relationship with God. Seeing our children pray gives us peace. They know their Father, the One who loves and cares so much for them—even more than we do.

Finally

$\mathcal{P}$RAYER KEEPS ME IN better touch with the nations politically than the media. It keeps me in tune with the Sunday morning sermons. Prayer holds my children in my heart daily and my friends just a thought away.

There are only so many hours in the day. We all have to decide how we will spend them. In reflection, I am very thankful that God drew me to prayer as a life goal on that evening of my birthday when I was a young single mom. I still want to learn more.

Whatever time you can spend in prayer, the *benefits* to you and your family will be wonderful. As we pray for our own lives, our children's lives, and make a difference somewhere in this world outside our four walls, the results will bring healing and restoration in our homes and nation.

Jesus said in Matthew 6:6 (KJV) that when we pray, we should go into our closet and shut the door behind us. Your prayer closet may be your bedroom, favorite chair in the living room, or even the bathtub. It is wherever you can best shut out the busyness of this world.

I truly encourage you to set aside *a time to pray*.

Seven Principles of Prayer

1. You do the praying. Make room for God to answer as He wills.

2. Time spent reading the Bible and being in God's presence increases your level of authority over Satan.

3. Do not pray because you seek the approval of man. Be willing to see the kingdom of God expand without personal recognition.

4. When you have an urgency to pray, yet do not know what it pertains to, the only thing you can do is to keep yielding to the Holy Spirit.

5. When God calls you to a season of prayer, you must be willing to carry the burden without the help of others.

6. When God speaks clearly to you to pray, it does not matter if you understand any details. The question is: "Do you love Him and His people enough to respond?"

7. Pray as though you are a soldier in a war, not a lady in distress. Push back the darkness for others until they see truth for themselves.

Further Information About Elaine Bond's Programs

Homemaking Schools

Elaine Bond's handbooks, *Home with a Heart*, serve as an inspiration for a program she taught first from her home and then in conjunction with The Salvation Army in the Niagara Region of Canada. It is now available for churches and ministries in other locations.

The program offers twelve-week Homemaking Schools accompanied by mentoring support to single mothers or any woman in need. The mothers are taught specific routines that Elaine developed, followed by daily goals to put them into practice. The result is in a well-organized, clean home with laundry completed, meals planned, routines for children, finances and paperwork organized, guidance with home business or other employment choices, and—yes, even time for mom. The *Home with a Heart* handbooks become a life-long resource for moms.

Home with a Heart

- ✑ *The Story Behind Home with a Heart*
- ✑ Planning for Success
- ✑ Handbook 1: *Organizing Your Household*
- ✑ Handbook 2: *Finances & Paperwork*
- ✑ Handbook 3: *Cooking Made Easy*
- ✑ Handbook 4: *Recipes Made Easy*
- ✑ Handbook 5: *Time for Mom*
- ✑ Handbook 6: *Hobbies*
- ✑ Handbook 7: *Parenting*
- ✑ Handbook 8: *Home Business & Job Search*

Local and national recognition of the program is growing. To start a Homemaking School in your organization, please visit: www.homewithaheart.org. *Home with a Heart* packages are available with everything you need to help you get started, including a well-developed Teacher Training Manual. Teacher-training conferences are offered as well.

Self-instructional Program

Home with a Heart is available as a self-instructional program or for one-on-one mentoring. To order the program please visit: www.homewithaheart.org.

The Story Behind Home with a Heart

This quick-reading book is the story of how Elaine built her home as a single mom, and then started to teach other women to do the same. It is a story of hope and faith, available as a gift item with *Home with a Heart* or may be ordered on its own. To order please visit: www.homewithaheart.org

A Time to Heal

Many women find it impossible to move forward due to unresolved pain in their lives. Elaine teaches and ministers in seminars called *A Time to Heal* so single moms can heal from past hurts and self-destructive patterns. A book by the same name is available for individuals or as an additional resource to each Homemaking School. To order please visit: www.homewithaheart.org.

Notes

Chapter 3—How to Move God's Hand

1. Author unknown.

Chapter 9—Moving God's Hand for Our Land

1. http://en.wikipedia.org/wiki/Centennial_Olympic_Park_
bombing (accessed February 26, 2007)

2. Article available online at www.en.wikipedia.org/wiki/
World_Trade_Center_bombing (accessed March 28, 2007).

Chapter 12—The Dance of Deception

1. Elaine Bond, *A Time to Heal* (Ontario, Canada: Home with
a Heart, 2005).

2. Poem available online at www.livingstonesnews.com/
modules.php?name=News&file=article&sid=540.

Chapter 15—Don't Give Up

1. Elaine Bond, *The Story Behind Home with a Heart* (Ontario,
Canada: Home with a Heart, 1999).